Eco-Prediction

Collecting Data

Diana Noonan

Publishing Credits

Editor
Sara Johnson

Editorial Director
Emily R. Smith, M.A.Ed.

Editor-in-Chief
Sharon Coan, M.S.Ed.

Creative Director
Lee Aucoin

Publisher
Rachelle Cracchiolo, M.S.Ed.

Image Credits

Teacher Created Materials

5301 Oceanus Drive
Huntington Beach, CA 92649-1030
http://www.tcmpub.com
ISBN 978-0-7439-0907-5
© 2009 Teacher Created Materials, Inc.
Reprinted 2012

Table of Contents

Help Needed

Hurry! There are 2 **ecosystems** that need your help. The experts have been called in. First, they will collect data. Then, they will use that data to make **predictions** about the problems. Lastly, they will plan ways to help the ecosystems.

Let's join them. First, you will collect and study data about a stream.

Data

Data is information. Data can be shown in tables, charts, and graphs.

Claymount Stream

Claymount Stream used to be a favorite place for people to fish. Children fished there using worms for bait. Adults enjoyed fly fishing. But now no one goes there. There are few fish left.

A Fishy Tale

"Five years ago, I could go fishing and come home with 3 good fish. Over the last few years, I have caught fewer fish. Now, I don't go to Claymount Stream because the fish just don't bite anymore."

A quote from Tom, a local Claymount Stream fisherman

Where Are the Fish?

Claymount Fishing Club members look at the results of their yearly fishing contest. They are worried. Where have all the fish gone?

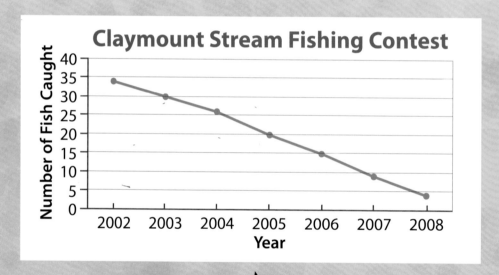

Claymount Stream Fishing Contest

LET'S EXPLORE MATH

Look at the fishing club competition results. Use the line graph to figure out the missing data in this chart.

Year	2002	2003	2004	2005	2006	2007	2008
Fish Caught	34		26		15		4

The people of Claymount are worried about Claymount Stream's ecosystem. The fishing club studies the **food chain** of the stream's ecosystem to see how fewer fish might change the life of the stream.

Claymount Stream Food Chain

Call in the Expert

The mayor of Claymount calls Mei Chan to help. Ms. Chan is a park **ranger**. She studies a map of the stream to see what might be causing the problems. Then she predicts some reasons for the drop in the number of fish. She makes a star diagram of her predictions.

Dropping Numbers of Fish

Waste from the dairy factory raising the temperature of the stream

Animal waste from dairy farms polluting the stream

Waste from the dairy factory polluting the stream

Soil and mud from the mill seeping into the stream

Too many people fishing in the stream

Ms. Chan will collect data on Claymount Stream. She also needs data on the stream's ecosystem. This will help her find answers.

Claymount Stream Map

dairy farm

dairy factory

town

mill

reserve

The Mill

The Claymount Mill turns grain into flour. Water from the stream is used to create power for machines at the mill. To get the water, the mill is built right on the stream bank. This could cause the bank to erode. Mud and soil may slip into the stream.

Collecting Data

Water Temperature

First, Ms. Chan tests the stream's water temperature every day for a week. Then she tests the water temperature of 3 nearby streams. She makes a table of her data and **compares** the results. The water temperatures are almost the same. So she **concludes** that water temperature is not causing the problem.

Temperature Results

Stream	Average May temperatures in degrees Celsius
Wattle Stream	12.3°C
Luke Stream	13.1°C
Chattel Stream	11.2°C
Claymount Stream	11.9°C

LET'S EXPLORE MATH

Look at the average temperatures for the 4 streams.

a. Round each temperature to the nearest degree Celsius.

b. Create a table ordering these temperatures from highest to lowest.

Clean Water?

Then Ms. Chan tests Claymont Stream's water to see how much soil is in it. The water is clear. So the mill is not the reason why fewer fish are in the stream.

Next, Ms. Chan tests how clean the water is. The results are normal for a stream. **Pollution** does not seem to be a problem.

Stream Life

Animal Life

Ms. Chan also collects data on the animal life in the stream. She swims in a part of the stream and counts any fish or frogs she sees. Then Ms. Chan uses a net to catch tadpoles. She counts them and puts them back.

Ms. Chan also studies insects at the stream. She puts her data in a table.

Insect Results

Insect	Sample 1	Sample 2	Average
water boatmen	22	19	20.5
pond skaters	18	21	19.5
dragonflies	1	1	1

Ms. Chan records all her animal studies on a bar graph.

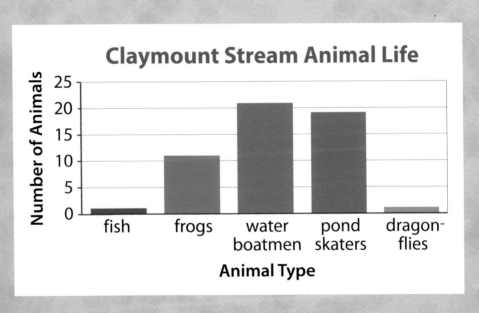

Claymount Stream has lots of water insects. Frog numbers are also high. There are not enough fish to eat tadpoles and insects. But dragonfly numbers are decreasing. This is because frogs eat dragonflies. When there are more frogs, there are fewer dragonflies.

Plant Life

Ms. Chan collects data on the plants in the stream. Plants grow quickly in Claymount Stream because there are few fish to feed on them. Ms. Chan predicts that the plants will clog the stream. This may cause flooding in the future.

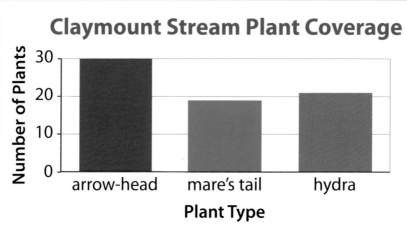

Predictions Can Become Solutions

Ms. Chan **reviews** her star diagram and looks over her data. Water temperature is not a problem for the stream. There is no pollution from animal waste or factories. And the water is clear of soil and mud. So Ms. Chan concludes that the problem is over-fishing. People catch too many fish from Claymount Stream.

Ms. Chan tells the Claymount Fishing Club to **ban** fishing for 3 years. After that, people can only catch smaller amounts of fish. She also says that some stream plants should be taken out. This will keep the stream flowing properly.

The Future

   Claymount Fishing Club members put up "No Fishing" signs. Then, they take some water plants out of the stream. This keeps the stream flowing.

   Over time, the ecosystem of Claymount Stream will get better. In a few years, people will enjoy fishing again.

Problems in the Woodland

Now you will need to collect and study data about Mainsville Woods.

Mainsville Reserve is part of Mainsville Woods. A reserve is a place where animals and plants are **protected**. They cannot be hunted. Many deer, birds, and insects live there. Many people from Mainsville Nature Club visit the reserve.

Mainsville Woods

Bird Study

Members of the Mainsville Nature Club study 3 **species** (SPEE-seez) of birds in the reserve. They count the number of each species they see. They do this for 5 years. Then they make graphs of their data, like the graph below.

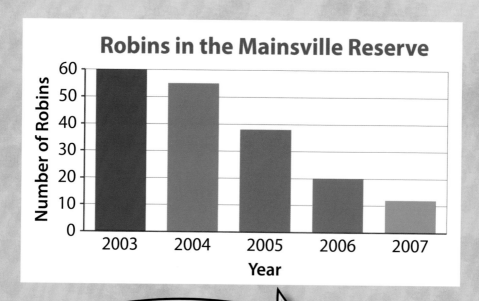

Robins in the Mainsville Reserve

LET'S EXPLORE MATH

Look at the graph above.

a. Between which 2 years did robin numbers drop the most?

b. About how many robins were there in 2004?

c. Did the number of robins increase in any year?

d. About how many more robins were there in 2004 than in 2007?

Bird Predictions

The bird watchers look at the graphs. They predict that the number of birds will keep dropping. Are numbers dropping in the reserve only? What is the number of birds in Mainsville Woods?

The bird watchers begin to count the birds in the woods. Their data is surprising. There are many more birds outside the reserve than inside!

You Predict

Can you predict why bird numbers are dropping in the reserve? Perhaps you need more data before you can think of an **accurate** answer.

Expert Help

What is happening to the birds in the reserve? Expert help is needed. The members of the nature club ask wildlife scientist, Alex Brown, for help.

Mr. Brown needs to collect data. He chooses 2 areas of the woods to study. He calls them *Area A* (in the reserve) and *Area B* (outside the reserve).

Insect Alert!

The **entomologists** (en-tuh-MOL-uh-jists) are also worried. If the number of birds is dropping, will the number of insects increase or decrease?

Plant Data

First, Mr. Brown studies plants. He uses string to mark out a grid in each area he studies. He collects data on how much space each plant type in the grid takes up.

This is one of the areas Mr. Brown studies outside the reserve.

This is one of the areas Mr. Brown studies inside the reserve.

Plant Results

Mr. Brown looks at his data on Area A and Area B. There are fewer plants inside the reserve than outside it. This difference is causing the number of birds to drop. Most woodland birds eat seeds and fruits. Clear ground means less food for birds to eat. But this also raises a new question—why are there fewer plants in the reserve?

Arrowwood Shrubs in Mainsville Woods

	Inside Reserve	Outside Reserve
Number of Shrubs	||	||||| ||

LET'S EXPLORE MATH

Look at the table above to see how many arrowwood shrubs Mr. Brown counts inside and outside of the reserve.

a. Create a **frequency table** showing in numbers how many arrowwood shrubs Mr. Brown counts.

b. Create a bar graph to display this data.

Animal Data

Deer Data

Then, Mr. Brown collects data on the deer inside and outside of the reserve. The deer outside the reserve are hunted twice a year. But the deer inside the reserve are not hunted.

Mr. Brown also studies what the deer eat. The deer eat grass, small trees, and shrubs. They enjoy eating the new growth on plants.

Animal Invasion?

Mr. Brown looks at his data so far. There are more deer in the reserve eating plants. This makes large areas of clear ground. The clear ground allows other animals to move into the reserve, and some of these animals hunt birds.

Mr. Brown makes a flow chart to show the problem.

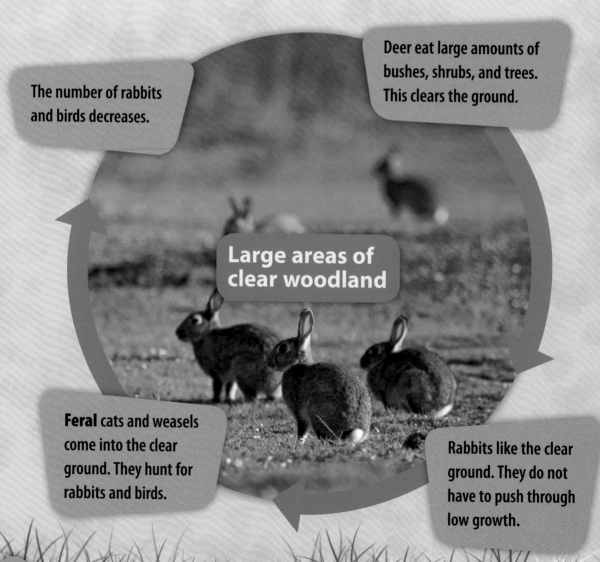

Deer eat large amounts of bushes, shrubs, and trees. This clears the ground.

The number of rabbits and birds decreases.

Large areas of clear woodland

Feral cats and weasels come into the clear ground. They hunt for rabbits and birds.

Rabbits like the clear ground. They do not have to push through low growth.

Insect Data

Mr. Brown then collects data on insects. He studies areas inside and outside of the reserve. He counts the number of sites that have insect eggs. Then he counts the number of insects he sees.

LET'S EXPLORE MATH

This is the data collected by Mr. Brown.

Insect Data

	Numbers of insect egg sites	Number of insects
Area A	15	45
Area B	41	65

Create 2 bar graphs. The first should show the number of insect egg sites in Area A and Area B. The second should show the number of insects in these sites.

Mr. Brown concludes that there are fewer insect eggs in the reserve. There are not enough plants for insects to lay their eggs on. But the insect numbers in the reserve are not as low as they could be because there are fewer birds to eat the insects. This means that lack of plant life for the insect eggs is a large part of the problem. The birds do not have enough to feed on!

Predictions for Problems

Mr. Brown looks at his data. Too many deer are eating plants in the reserve. They eat the small plants that the birds use for food. The insects lay their eggs on these plants, too. The clear ground also means that other animals come into the reserve and eat the birds.

Something has to be done about the number of deer in the reserve. But the Mainsville Nature Club does not want the deer to be hunted.

Deer on the Move!

The club wants the bird life in the reserve to be healthy. The entomologists want the insect life to be healthy also. So many of the deer are caught. Then they are taken to another area of woodland.

Thanks to Mr. Brown's data and research, the wildlife in Mainsville Reserve will grow stronger.

Save the Birds!

Jacinta has a flowering dogwood tree in her backyard. She loves to watch the beautiful birds that come to eat the berries. Her neighbor, Mr. Hodges, wants Jacinta to cut down the tree because the berries are falling into his garden.

Jacinta knows Mr. Hodges also likes watching birds. She decides to count the number of birds so she can create a graph that shows how many birds would not visit their yards if she cut the tree down. She thinks this will convince Mr. Hodges to let her keep the tree.

Birds in the Tree

Day of the Week	Number of Birds
Monday	卌 卌 卌 II
Tuesday	卌 卌 卌 IIII
Wednesday	卌 卌 卌 卌
Thursday	卌 卌 卌 III
Friday	卌 卌 卌 卌 II
Saturday	卌 卌 卌 II
Sunday	卌 卌 卌 I

Solve It!

a. Draw a frequency table to show the number of birds (in numerals) that visit the tree each day for the week.

b. Use the data in the table to draw the graph that Jacinta creates to show Mr. Hodges.

c. Write 3 questions about the graph.

Glossary

accurate—correct

ban—to stop something because of an official order

compares—looks at the features of two or more things to see how they are the same or different

concludes—decides

ecosystems—systems of living things interacting with their environments

entomologists—scientists who study insects

feral—a domestic animal that has gone wild

food chain—a diagram that shows how energy (food) is passed from one organism to another; arrows show the direction of the energy flow

frequency table—a chart showing a set of events and how often the events occur

pollution—spoiling the environment through litter, waste, and so on

predictions—things that are said to happen in the future based on observations and experiences

protected—something that must not be harmed

ranger—a person whose job it is to look after a park or public area

reviews—looks at or shows again

species—a group of animals or plants with similar features

Index

Let's Explore Math

Page 6:

Year	2002	2003	2004	2005	2006	2007	2008
Fish Caught	34	30	26	20	15	9	4

Page 10:

a. Wattle Stream: 12°C; Luke Stream: 13°C; Chattel Stream: 11°C; Claymount Stream: 12°C

b.

Stream	Average May Temperatures
Luke Stream	13°C
Wattle Stream	12°C
Claymount Steam	12°C
Chattel Stream	11°C

Page 18:

a. Between 2005 and 2006 c. No

b. About 55 d. About 44

Page 22:

a.

	Number of Arrowwoods
Inside Reserve	2
Outside Reserve	7

b.

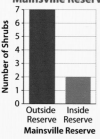

Page 25:

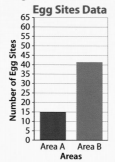
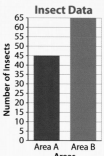

Problem-Solving Activity

a.

Day of the Week	Number of Birds
Monday	17
Tuesday	19
Wednesday	20
Thursday	18
Friday	22
Saturday	17
Sunday	16

b.

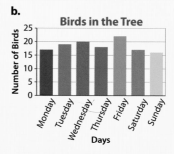

c. Graph questions will vary.